MW00777744

Blank

First Series: August 2021

Printed in the United States of America.

ISBN-13: 978-0-578-97307-4

I would like to say thank you to my family and all the people in my life who have inspired me and stood by me and challenged me.

Contents

Chapter 1

Introduction

"Every day is a chance to be better."
--Unknown

There are countless books about anxiety — some are complex, some are simple. My goal is to add a simple yet robust option for people to learn the easy strategies I use in my support groups and individual counseling sessions with people of all ages. The techniques in this book will assist in learning how to identify anxiety and unhealthy thinking patterns and how to implement methods to reduce and manage anxiety.

This book isn't written in clinical terms; I don't want to overwhelm you. The strategies and methods you'll discover in the next few pages are a way to start actively helping you address and manage anxiety, helping you work toward a happier and healthier way of coping and thinking.

I am sure many of you have already purchased endless books and talked to others about anxiety, and this self-help book is another one to add to your collection. Why do I make this assumption? Because as an anxious individual myself, I spent years searching for the same answers and learned when an individual is ready they will learn about and work through their anxiety. One can learn all the tools needed and have the awareness, but until one is ready to make the difference, the tools sit on a shelf.

I will keep the information as informative as I can so that you can learn why your anxiety is a big part of your life, how to recognize it, and how to reduce it. I also know if I write too much and try to explain too much it may overwhelm you, so I'll keep it to the point, with simplified explanations and methods you can use.

You will learn:

- To identify triggers of anxiety episodes
- To identify irrational thoughts and beliefs
- To identify sensory overload
- To identify how you feel during an anxiety attack
- To reduce and/or manage your anxiety
- To replace irrational thoughts and beliefs with healthy thoughts and beliefs

Use this book as a supplement if you are in therapy. **If anxiety is severe, professional assistance is your best approach.**

"Sometimes we're tested not to show our weakness but to discover our strengths."
--Suhani Jain

Q: What is anxiety?

An emotion characterized by feelings of fear, tension and worry. It is a reaction to stress. It is excessive worry and fear usually about everyday situations; an event or something with an uncertain outcome. The feelings are extreme and interfere with your daily life.

Q: What is the difference between normal anxiety and an anxiety disorder?

- **Normal anxiety**: Individuals experience anxiety as a reaction to an event or situation that occurs in our life and usually lasts for a short period of time. This anxiety does not affect your quality of life.
- **Anxiety disorder**: Recurring intrusive thoughts and/or concerns that do not go away. The fear and worry is present all the time, which can increase in intensity and frequency and affects your quality of life. This anxiety becomes overwhelming and surfaces for no reason. You may also find yourself avoiding situations out of worry.

Q: Why am I anxious?
- Genetics
- Brain chemistry
- Personality
- Ongoing stressful events
- Influenced by environmental factors

Q: What effects can anxiety disorders have?
Individuals can experience anxiety attacks, panic attacks, social isolation, depression, and challenging relationships, challenging a person's ability to work and perform routine activities.

Q: Will I be anxious my entire life?
Most people with an anxiety disorder will never completely be anxiety-free, but you can learn how to control it and reduce the intensity and frequency.

Next, we will briefly explain the different anxiety disorders.

"Don't be a victim of your negative thoughts."
--Unknown

Q: What anxiety diagnosis will help me use this workbook?

I don't address Agoraphobia, Other Phobias, and Obsessive-Compulsive Disorder because intense treatment is required for these diagnoses.

Generalized Anxiety Disorder is when an individual has excessive worry about events or activities, e.g., family, school, friends, work. These feelings occur most of the time with no specific trigger. This anxiety is difficult to control and is disproportionate to the fear.

Common symptoms include:
- Sleep disturbance
- Irritability
- Difficulty concentrating
- Muscle tension
- Weak or tired
- Sense of danger
- Increased heart rate
- Sweating
- Restlessness
- Chronic headaches

Panic Disorder is when an individual experiences uncontrollable, recurrent episodes of panic and fear within minutes of each other. There is no warning before the panic attacks occur and they are not always linked to a trigger, making them difficult to predict.

Common symptoms include:
- Pounding heart
- Shortness of breath
- Nausea
- Dizziness, lightheadedness
- Fear of losing control
- Numbness
- Chills
- Sweating
- Choking feeling
- Trembling
- Feeling detached from reality

What is Anxiety?

"Have patience. All things are difficult before they become easy."
--Saadi

Separation Anxiety Disorder is an individual's excessive worry about being away from their parents. The individual fears that something will happen to their parents and that they will never see them again. This is often seen in children, but also appears in adolescents when a stressor has occurred.

Common symptoms include:
- Extreme distress when separated from home or the attachment figure
- Persistent fear of being alone
- Frequent physical complaints while separated from the attachment figure

Social Anxiety Disorder is an individual's persistent fear of social situations, or a situation where the individual may need to perform.

Common symptoms include:
- Fear of meeting other people
- Easily embarrassed
- Feeling insecure and out of place
- Fear of having to speak in public
- Fear of being the center of attention
- Fear of being criticized

Unspecified Anxiety Disorder -   Anxious feelings or fears followed by physical symptoms associated with anxiety. When a person can't explain why they are anxious; they have an anxious feeling followed by physical symptoms associated with anxiety.

When an individual exhibits symptom of two or more kinds of anxiety and does not meet the full criteria for a particular anxiety disorder he/she will be diagnosed **with Unspecified Anxiety Disorder.** Although a person does not meet the criteria the symptoms can cause significant distress. This diagnose can be challenging to diagnose and treat because of the uncertainty of the cause.

Symptoms include:
Short tempered / irritable
Sleep problems
Avoidance of situations
Detachment from friends and/or family
Nervousness
Overreacting
Extreme anxiety
Panic attacks
Difficulty concentrating
Less/low motivation

What is your anxiety?

"Worry doesn't empty tomorrow of its sorrows; it empties today of its strengths."
--Corrie ten Boom

List your anxiety(ies): Your symptoms?

_____

_____

_____

_____

_____

_____

_____

_____

_____

_____

_____

_____

_____

_____

_____

_____

_____

_____

_____

Chapter 3

What are Negative Core Beliefs?

Q: What are core beliefs?

Negative core beliefs are beliefs (assumptions/expectations) we think about ourselves (our identity), others, and the world. These beliefs are also our security, insecurity, self doubt, and validation of ourselves. They are also assumptions that influence our behavior, how we see others and situations.

Q: Why do I think this way?

These beliefs can start in childhood, early adulthood, and from traumatic experiences. They are learned from experience. Negative beliefs about yourself can stem from early childhood criticism from others, including high expectations from others. Negative core beliefs of others usually develop from witnessing or experiencing traumatic experiences and relating these experiences to the world.

Q: How do negative core beliefs affect me?

Negative core beliefs can impact feelings, behaviors, and our perception of how we should be and expect others to be. **These beliefs can lead a person to negative self talk that can lead to cognitive distortions, which is irrational thinking.**

Q: Can I change my negative core beliefs?

Yes, it is possible to change the negative beliefs. It will take work and can be challenging because these beliefs are embedded and formed in early life. You will need to recognize your patterns to determine the negative core beliefs.

Q: Are core beliefs and expectations similar?

Yes, when we project our negative core beliefs onto others we are expecting them to think and feel them the same way we do, and when they don't it creates a disconnect between people.

Q: What are unhealthy core beliefs?

A person's unhealthy core belief is a negative automatic assumption about themselves and others.

I am a loser	No one likes me	I am worthless
I am no good	I am bad	I am unlovable
I can't do anything right	I am not smart	I am ugly
I am weak	I will be lonely	Nothing is ever easy
I am a failure	I don't belong	I always doing something wrong
I cannot trust anyone	I am not in control	I am inadequate
I can't trust myself	It's not right to show emotion	I will be alone
I do things wrong	I should know better	

I am not thin, therefore no one thinks I'm pretty.
If I don't meet others' expectations, I am not a good person.
I am not rich, therefore I am not successful.
I am not smart and can't do anything.
People who don't agree with me are difficult and not nice.
People who don't work hard are lazy.
If I don't do well in school, I will never succeed.
If someone doesn't call me back that means they don't like me.

What are Negative Core Beliefs?

"When a negative thought enters your mind, think three positive ones.
Train yourself to flip the script."
--Unknown

Q: What are healthy core beliefs?

I am a good person	I am lovable	I deserve to be happy
I learned from the situation	I can express myself	I am in control
I can trust people I want to trust	I am worthwhile	I can make mistakes
I did my best	I have courage	I choose to be positive
I am good with who I am	I am important	I trust my choices

Q: What else can negative core beliefs do to me?

A person may find it difficult to trust other people; may be aggressive; may, without realizing it, always put their needs on the back burner and take care of others; may feel inadequate in relationships; and can be very confrontational.

Q: Can you give an example of a negative core belief and what the positive belief could be?

Negative
June: "I am always a failure."
Situation: Believes she is a failure because she forgot to complete a project on time
Feeling: Is depressed
Behavior: Her depression stops her from making any changes to her negative belief

Bob: "I have no luck."
Situation: Bob didn't get a job he interviewed for and feels he has no luck
Feeling: Is depressed
Behavior: His depression stops him from making changes to his negative belief

Positive
June: "I try my best."
Situation: I didn't get enough sleep and couldn't concentrate
Feeling: Disappointed
Behavior: Won't stay up late when projects are due

Bob: "I trust my choices."
Situation: I applied for a job that I did not qualify for
Feeling: Disappointed
Behavior: Will learn from the situation and stay focused

What are Negative Core Beliefs?

"Look for something positive each day, even if some days you have to look a little harder."
--Unknown

The following situation is an example you can use to help you with recognizing your core beliefs and how they trigger your anxiety.

Situation: Bill's wife Debra tells Bill she feels that he doesn't love her the same way as she does and needs him to express it to her more. She tells him he doesn't say it enough and feels alone and hurt. Bill responds to Debra and tells her that he does not need to always tell her. Debra replies, "I don't believe you," and the conversation turns into an argument.

Debra's core belief : If I don't express my emotions it means I am not lovable

↓

Debra's expectation: People need to validate their love to feel loved

↓

Irrational Thought: Fortunetelling, catastrophizing, all-or-nothing thinking

↓

Anxiety Trigger: Bill doesn't tell Debra he loves her on a regular basis. His beliefs are different than Debra's and because of this her anxiety was triggered.

Core Beliefs

List your negative core beliefs:

_____

_____

_____

_____

_____

_____

_____

_____

_____

Think back and explore when each belief originated:

_____

_____

_____

_____

_____

_____

_____

_____

_____

_____

Core Beliefs

Replace the negative core beliefs with positive core beliefs.

_____

_____

_____

_____

_____

_____

_____

_____

_____

_____

_____

_____

_____

_____

_____

_____

_____

_____

_____

Chapter 4

Expectations and Assumptions

Q: What are expectations?

Expectations are the strong belief that something will happen or should be a certain way. More than anything else, our expectations determine our reality, and our expectations also impact those around us. In a self-fulfilling prophecy, people may rise or fall depending on our expectations and beliefs.

Of course we all have them, and at times we blame them for our disappointments, frustrations, and conflict. However, sometimes we need to sit and self-reflect what our expectations are. We need to revisit our core beliefs and either learn to be more flexible in our beliefs or lower the expectations of others to find a healthy balance.
It is also important for the people in our lives to know what your expectations are. Don't assume they know - they aren't you. Do we self-sabotage, can we learn to be more flexible in understanding, can we lower some of our expectations to avoid the disappointment when others don't meet them?

Expectations can come from our core beliefs and can be projected onto others. When they fail to meet our expectations, we have a problem. From our perspective we assume they don't care, they are not respectful, they don't appreciate us, they are hurtful, they are selfish, and whatever else one comes up with. Sometimes these reasons are valid and sometimes they aren't. It's when they aren't true that creates tension, resentment, disappointment, anger and hurt. An easy solution is to recognize your expectations, as they can contribute to your anxiety.

Adjusting expectations:

Don't expect people to think like you.
Don't expect people to treat you how you want to be treated.
Don't expect people to know what you mean.
Don't expect people to believe the same as you do.

Additionally, what happens to you when you project your expections onto others:

Feel let down
Feel hurt
Feel angry
Feel disappointed
Feel misunderstood
Feel unheard
Feel unloved

Expectations and Assumptions

"The 3 C's of life: Choices, Chances, Changes. You must make the choice, to take a chance, if you want anything in life to change."
--Zig Ziglar

List your expectations of others:

_____

_____

_____

_____

_____

_____

_____

_____

Replace the high expectations with rational expectations:

_____

_____

_____

_____

_____

_____

_____

_____

_____

People spend a lot of time worrying about what other people think of them, and about their own worthiness - are we enough? When people think like this, they spend part of their life comparing themselves to others, people-pleasing, and proving. The only person that can let go of this is you.

Know your love language:
Gifts/tokens of affection – gifts, thoughtfulness
Quality time together – one-on-one time
Physical touch – touch and body language
Words of affirmation - affirm, listen actively, appreciate, empathize
Acts of service - action phrases

_____

_____

_____

Address shame:
Talk about it.
Who are you when you feel shame?

_____

_____

How do you protect yourself?

_____

_____

Authentic or inauthentic self:

It's a conscious choice of how we want to live and how we want to be seen.
Think of yourself and define what authenticity means to you. Who am I supposed to be, and who am I?

_____

_____

_____

Reflect

"Life is a one time offer. Live it well."
--Unknown

_____

_____

_____

_____

_____

_____

_____

_____

_____

_____

_____

_____

_____

_____

_____

_____

_____

_____

_____

Chapter 5

What is Irrational Thinking?

Q: What is irrational thinking?
Irrational thoughts or beliefs are distorted perceptions of reality that present in a negative way and occur under emotional distress. These thoughts are emotional reactions to situations.

Q: Can these thoughts affect your life?
Yes. They will increase anxiety, depression and stress.

Q: Does everyone have irrational thought patterns?
Yes, we all do, but someone with an anxiety disorder struggles with looking at a situation logically and continues to think the worst. Most people with anxiety have irrational thought patterns. They are aware of this but can't control their thoughts. There are also times these thoughts are automatic, a habit.

Q: How do I determine if my thought patterns are affecting my quality of life and making me anxious?
To help determine if thought patterns are affecting your quality of life, ask yourself the following questions:

How often do you find fault in everyone else? Is it almost all the time, or just some of the time? If it's almost all the time, it is likely affecting your quality of life. Now, ask yourself how it can be *all of the time*. Is everyone else always wrong? Do people always wrong you?

The goal is to recognize your irrational thinking patterns and to remind yourself when your thoughts are irrational. "Why am I they thinking this way? What do I gain by thinking this way? How do I feel when I think this way?" How about your expectations and assumptions? These also play a large role in anxiety. Once you begin to recognize your irrational thoughts, you will start to think in a healthier way and you are on your way to a calmer self.

Q: How can I can make this work for me?
By working at it, recognizing your patterns, and committing to changing the thought pattern(s) when you are ready.

On the next page, you will find common irrational thinking patterns. After you have read each one, determine those that apply to you. Check them off and date the bottom of the page. Your goal is to recognize irrational thinking patterns and to replace them with healthier ones. Occasionally, revisit the irrational thinking checklist to see how far you have come. It's great to see the progress you are making.

"If you want change, focus on changing yourself, not others."
--Unknown

❑ **All-or-nothing thinking:** An individual views everything in the extreme. It's either right or wrong, true or untrue. Rarely does one see shades of grey. This is the inability to see alternatives to a problem.

❑ **Overgeneralization:** An individual takes one experience and believes this will always occur. For example, you're not invited to a party, therefore you'll never be invited to any parties.

❑ **Catastrophizing or minimizing:** An individual either exaggerates or minimizes a situation. For example:

Catastrophizing: Billy bumped into another student during lunch and the student's apple fell on the floor. The student told Billy it was okay and that it was just an accident, but Billy got so upset over it that he thought about it for days.

Minimizing: Mary beat the track record at school and won an award. Afterward, she gave a short speech and people applauded her. However, Mary complained that she was so nervous that her speech was dumb.

❑ **Emotional reasoning:** An individual views that how they feel is what defines them. For example, Jane feels dumb, so she's convinced that she is dumb, even though she does well in school.

❑ **"Should" statement:** This statement (also includes "ought" or "must") usually induces feelings of guilt; the motivation for doing something is based on what others think. This thinking usually leads to procrastination.

"You can't always choose what happens to you, but you can always choose how you feel about it."
--Danielle Laporte

❏ **Labeling and mislabeling:** An individual does the opposite of overgeneralization.
Labeling - you label yourself: "I'm dumb."
Mislabeling - you label someone else's behavior: "She's a weirdo."

❏ **Personalization:** An individual believes they're the cause of a negative event. For example, if Mary doesn't call you back, she must not like you.

❏ **Fortune-telling:** An individual tends to predict that things will turn out badly.

❏ **Disqualifying the positives:** An individual doesn't give themselves credit when they do something positive and/or good. They feel it's not deserved.

❏ **Negative thoughts:** An individual only looks at the negative side of an event, situation, or action. For example, you lost your lunch money, but you had a great day with friends. Your focus is on the lost money.

After reading the thought patterns, check off the one(s) that you do most or all of the time. Once you have completed this, the next step is to raise awareness so you can recognize when it occurs. You will learn to automatically recognize when the irrational thought is occurring and eventually challenge the thought.

Notes:

_____

_____

_____

_____

"Not all storms come to disrupt your life. Some come to clear your path."
--Unknown

This exercise will help you think more rationally about an assumption and/or rule that may be harmful thinking.

Think about a scenario when you felt bad about your thought. Write a short description about the situation.

Next, identify the assumption/thought that occurred. How did you react?

Challenge yourself and ask yourself what happened in your life to acquire this thought, how/when did you learn it, and what encouraged you to believe it?

Once these questions are asked, you are going to compare the advantages and disadvantages of thinking this way.

Use self talk to stop the irrational thoughts. Make yourself aware of these irrational thoughts as they occur. Keeping a daily log can also be helpful. The following is an example to assist you in finding the method that works for you so you can learn to replace the unhealthy thoughts with healthier thoughts.

The following is an example for you so you can use the worksheet at the end of the workbook.

The situation	What negative thought did you have	Choose an alternative healthy thought
"I am so nervous speaking in public. I know people are thinking how awful I am presenting."	Focusing on the negative	"I am more confident and a better speaker than I realize. I've always done well, and people have told me this."
"I'll never feel content. I will always worry about everything."	Overgeneralizing	"I can be laid back and be relaxed. I can choose to let go of my worries."
"My stomachache must mean something is wrong with me."	Catastrophic thinking	"Many reasons my stomach can hurt. Most of the time it's my food choices and it goes away."
"If I can't be in control I can't function during the day."	Should	"I can only control my actions and reactions. I can not control how other people react and act."

Advantages of your negative thought patterns:

_____

_____

_____

_____

Disadvantages of your negative thought patterns:

_____

_____

_____

_____

"Happiness is not by chance, but by choice."
--Jim Rohn

What irrational thinking/behavior looks like:

Thoughts affect both your feelings and your body sensations, which, in turn, affect your overall behavior towards situations.

For example, thinking, "nobody likes me" can create a feeling of anxiety (feelings) around other people, which, in turn, may cause sweaty palms (bodily sensations) resulting in withdrawing from your friends (behavior), resulting in feeling left out.

Thoughts

"Nobody likes me"
"I always make mistakes"
"They are mad at me"

Behavior

Withdraw from friends
Stop doing what you enjoy

Feelings

Sad
Anxious

Body Sensations
No energy
Tired
Tense

Irrational Thinking Patterns

"I can't always control my thoughts, but I can choose how I respond to them."
--David Cuschieri

How often do you find yourself stuck in these thought patterns? How often do you recognize the thought patterns that are occurring? Do you ruminate/overthink?

_____

_____

_____

_____

_____

_____

_____

_____

_____

_____

_____

_____

_____

_____

_____

_____

Check In With Your Progress

Some days may still be a challenge and you will get to that better place!

Notes to self: What have I learned?

_____

_____

_____

_____

_____

_____

_____

_____

_____

_____

_____

_____

_____

_____

_____

_____

_____

_____

_____

_____

_____

_____

Chapter 6

What is Sensory Overload?

Why have I included sensory overload? Because it is important to recognize it if it happens to you. Individuals with anxiety, ADHD, Autism, PTSD, and sensory processing disorder experience sensory overload, and at times, individuals with anxiety will automatically think they are anxious and not recognize that they are experiencing sensory overload.

Q: What is sensory overload?
As you know, we have five senses: Sight, Sound, Smell, Taste, and Touch. When one or more senses has too much going on, your brain is overstimulated and cannot process all of it, which leads to sensory overload.
- Clothes being itchy - Touch
- Lights may be too bright - Sight
- Food textures cause gagging – Taste, Smell
- Sounds are too loud - Sound
- Touches are uncomfortable - Touch

Q: What are the symptoms of sensory overload?
- Agitation
- Irritability
- Discomfort and/or restlessness
- Feeling of over-excitedness
- Fear, stress and/or anxiety
- Sensitivity to material/things against your skin
- Need to cover your ears
- Need to cover your eyes
- Difficulty focusing

Q: What does sensory overload feel like?
You attend an event or a party, or are in a classroom, and the people and/or music are loud. The loudness will trigger symptoms of sensory overload (overstimulation of the brain) which makes it difficult to process information, and the individual may not be able to function. This can trigger their anxiety.

Q: What is it like for someone with anxiety?
Someone with anxiety will relate how anxious they feel at a party because they do not like the loud noises, so they avoid going to parties. However, it's not the anxiety that is preventing them from going to the party, it is the loud noise that is difficult to process - but their automatic thought is that it is their anxiety. Here the audio sensory overload is the trigger for their anxiety. If the music wasn't loud, they would attend the party and not feel anxious and not associate loud noises with the reason for their anxiety.

"You are the greatest project you will ever work on."
--Unknown

Sensory Overload

Take some time and think about the daily life situations and/or events in which you experience anxiety, and recognize if sensory overload was occurring.

Sight:

_____

_____

_____

Sound:

_____

_____

_____

Smell:

_____

_____

_____

Taste:

_____

_____

_____

Touch:

_____

_____

_____

Example of ineffective communication and listening:

Cathy is entering the seventh grade. She has always done well in school, and has many friends. She participates in sports and is part of a dance group. Cathy's grades, however, have started to decline, and she's having problems with her friend group. She begins to complain about the kids in school and one of her teachers. She isn't sleeping well, and is getting up late for school.

Mom: Hi, Cathy. How was school today?
Cathy: It was okay. Gotta go to my room; talk to you later.

An hour later, Mom knocks on Cathy's door.

Mom: Are you finished with your homework?
Cathy: No, not yet, talking with some friends. I'll start my homework in a few minutes.

Mom notices Cathy is distracted.

Mom: Are you okay, Cathy?
Cathy: Sure, Mom, I'm good.

The next day, the school counselor calls Mom and tells her Cathy's grades are dropping, and teachers have noticed she's been eating lunch alone.

Mom: Hi, Cathy. How was school today?
Cathy: Stupid. Middle School is stupid.

Mom: I received a call from your guidance counselor and we talked about your grades and how you've been eating alone.
Cathy: Yeah, my friends are stupid. School is hard and I'm getting all confused with the homework.

Mom: Girls can be mean. Just ignore them. What's going on with your grades? Do you need a tutor for school? If you do, let me know and I'll look into it for you. For now, no phone use until your grades get better.

Cathy: That's not fair. What if my friends text me and I miss something?
Mom: It's not the end of the world if you don't text them back. Do some reading - you need to get your grades back up.

How do you Communicate?

"Lack of communication ruins everything, because instead of knowing how the other person is feeling, we just assume."
--Unknown

Not to worry; effective listening and communication are not always easy. There are many factors that go into miscommunication, including feeling shy, scared, or angry, all of which break down effective communication.

The inability to listen, and its associated complications, can also cause distress in family situations that would easily be handled if we knew how to better communicate with each other. Complications may include: differences in learning styles, cultural differences, and psychological disorders.

By the way, if you are wondering why I've included this in the book – it's because it is important. Communication can decrease one's anxiety, and the other person will be able to hear and understand you better. Once you start conversations with the "I" statements, you will experience how healthy most conversations can be. Your thought patterns will be challenged when you communicate this way and your defensiveness and over-explaining will slowly diminish because your confidence and self esteem will be stronger.

Healthy word choices and other ways you can communicate:

Learn to use "I" statements: *** Very important! It will change situations dramatically when you start off with "I".
"I am hurt when this happens." "I am unsure how to help you." "I want you to tell me what that feels like." "I want you to trust me." "I am here for you when you need me." "I don't understand, so help me understand. I will listen to you. I am unsure how to help you."

Minimize/Avoid "You" statements. This is a great way to start an argument and cause tension, and the other person will already be on the defense. Be very careful here. "You never listen when I tell you to do something." "You always forget." "You don't try hard enough." "You are always late."

Learn how to engage in active listening: Understand the information, including the words and emotions an individual is trying to communicate - it shows them you are interested and engaged. Provide positive feedback. Let them speak without interrupting.

Avoid blaming others.

Learn to use the 10 second rule. If you feel angry, let the other person know that you're going to take a 10 second break before you talk to them. If you're still angry, let the other person know you need a few minutes to gather your thoughts.

Learn how to validate feelings: Don't disqualify how you feel or how others feel. You are not them, and they are not you.

On the next page, you will find an example of good communication skills.

Example of effective communication and listening:

Mom: Hi, Cathy. How are you?
Cathy: I'm okay. Gotta go to my room; talk to you later.

Mom: Hold on, sweetie, can we catch up for a few minutes and then you can go up to your room?
Cathy: Okay, I guess I have a few minutes. Why, is something wrong?

Mom: Nothing is wrong, it's just that we are so busy all the time and I want to hear how things are going and share a funny story with you.
Cathy: Okay. School was the same. Nothing interesting. Oh, wait, John got hit by a book today and broke his nose. Tracy got into a fight with her best friend and they called each other some bad names.

Mom: Goodness, that's a busy day. How did you feel about all of this?
Cathy: It's school, it's drama, it doesn't affect me because they aren't in my group. Anyway, I'm going up to my room now.

The next day, the school counselor calls Mom and tells her Cathy's grades are dropping, and teachers have noticed she's been eating lunch alone.

Mom: Hi, Cathy. How are you? How was your day?
Cathy: Stupid. Middle School is stupid.

Mom: I'm sorry you're feeling this way. I received a call from your guidance counselor and we talked about your grades and how you've been eating alone.
Cathy: Yeah, my friends are stupid. School is hard and I'm getting all confused with the homework.

Mom: Cathy, I can't tell you that this stuff won't happen, and that you won't be hurt, but I can tell you that worrying about it can affect you in unhealthy ways. How about this - settle in, have a snack, rest a while, and when you're ready we can sit together and talk about what you're going through and how it's making you feel. If you like, I'll share some of my experiences in life if it'll help you understand things a little better. I'm going to leave the choice up to you. Let me know.

Cathy: I like that plan, mom. Thanks. Let me just rest and do a few things.

The next page contains a few tips on keeping healthy communication going.

How do you Communicate?

Write down a situation of conflict:

_____

_____

_____

How did I communicate my feelings?

_____

_____

Do I recognize why I felt attacked?

_____

_____

Do I recognize a pattern that may cause the other person to feel attacked?

_____

_____

Did I approach the conversation with doubt?

_____

_____

How could I have communicated differently?

_____

_____

Was I flexible with understanding the perspective of the other person?

_____

_____

"I've got 99 problems and 86 of them are completely made up scenarios in my head that I'm stressing about for absolutely no logical reason."
--Unknown

Notes:

_____

_____

_____

_____

_____

_____

_____

_____

_____

Positive word of the day:

_____

_____

_____

Chapter 8

Recognize your Anxiety

"Stop being afraid of what could go wrong and think of what could go right."
--Unknown

It's time to learn about your anxiety. Upsetting events don't happen as often as you think, but when they do, they can be because people feel afraid, upset, uncertain, and helpless. There are different kinds of upsetting/confusing events. Let's learn about the anxiety-inducing events that you experience. Here you're going to recall anxious moments (unsettling events/situations when you became anxious) and answer the following questions:

When does it happen?

_____

_____

_____

Why does it happen?

_____

_____

_____

How often does it happen?

_____

_____

_____

How do you feel when it happens?

_____

_____

_____

How do you handle the situation?

_____

_____

Recognize your Anxiety

"A positive mind looks for ways it can done; A negative mind looks for ways it can't be done."
--Napoleon Hill

Now, down to the stuff that you can't let go, or maybe choose not to let go:

Are you living in the past? How? Why?

_____

_____

_____

_____

How often are you predicting the future? Why?

_____

_____

_____

_____

Do you really want to change? Yes, it's a question. Why? Because sometimes people are so comfortable with what they know that they are afraid to change because they can't imagine what it would be like to feel better. Well, decide if you want change - and do it.

_____

_____

_____

_____

_____

_____

Recognize your Anxiety

"No one ever injured their eyesight by looking on the bright side."
--Unknown

Your thoughts:

We sometimes think about negative things over and over again – this is unhealthy thinking. You can stop this by *recognizing* when you're repeating the negative thinking in your head.

List all the negative thoughts you repeat over and over. Recognize your patterns.

_____

_____

_____

_____

_____

_____

_____

_____

_____

_____

_____

_____

"Never give up, because great things take time."
--Curiano

Coping with your upsetting feelings:

When you experience an upsetting feeling, there are steps you can take to reduce the intensity. What are some things you do, and could do, to reduce the feelings?

What you do:

_____

_____

_____

_____

_____

_____

_____

What you can do instead:

_____

_____

_____

_____

_____

_____

_____

"Our attitude towards life determines life's attitude towards us."
--John Mitchell

When you find yourself overthinking, anxious, fearful, worried and stressed over situations (of course not dangerous situations), try the following methods and determine the one that works for you.

Thought-stopping: Use your watch or phone when this is occurring.

Set a timer for 20 minutes and tell yourself you are not going to worry, stress, wonder, or overthink for the next 20 minutes. Find something to do for the next 20 minutes. Once the timer goes off, allow yourself to go back to your "worry" and think about what was going on in your thoughts. Ask yourself the following:

What value did the irrational thought add to my quality of life?
What benefit did the irrational thought bring to my quality of life?

Open the door: Visual
Visualize a door. Open the door. Put your situation outside the door, and then close the door.
Set a timer for 20 minutes and tell yourself you are not going to worry, stress, wonder, or overthink for the next 20 minutes. Find something to do for the next 20 minutes. Once the timer goes off, allow yourself to go back to your "worry" and think about what was going on in your thoughts. Ask yourself the following:

What value did the irrational thought add to my quality of life?
What benefit did the irrational thought bring to my quality of life?

Name your anxiety:
Yes, name your anxiety. Think of a fun name and talk to your anxiety when you're feeling anxious. Ex: "Welcome back, Dory. I know you're anxious, and I know what is going on in your thoughts. You're scared, your stomach is uneasy, and your negative thoughts are extreme. I know this happens and I know you're not logical at the moment. I know you always get past this. I also know that as I challenge you this will get easier."

This method allows you to accept and embrace your anxiety. It is part of you. The more often you fight your anxiety and find fault with it, you actually increase your anxiety. It is more challenging to reduce the intensity and frequency of when it occurs. Let your anxiety be your friend – really, it works.

"Whenever I hear someone sigh, 'Life is hard,' I'm always tempted to ask, 'Compared to what?' "
--Sydney Harris

What is your Emotional Scale?

Here you are going to gauge your emotional scale. We are unique, and each scale rating works differently when it relates to how we react to a situation. Some of us may overreact because of our irrational thoughts. When this occurs, we become very anxious and the situation escalates to misunderstanding, conflict, arguments and disappointments. Think of a situation and rate your anxiety using the scale. Once you have determined your average number, you can challenge your number by asking yourself: Does my anxiety warrant the situation? Are my irrational thoughts the core of the anxiety?

Once you determine your number, you can recall this number when you find your anxiety affecting the situation and challenge the irrational thoughts.

First determine what the numbers mean to you.

Emotional Scale

1	2	3	4	5

1. Calm, no impact
2. Thinking about the situation; minimal reaction
3. Situation has elevated; you start to become defensive, tone gets louder, body language presents as guarded, angry, frustrated, anxious
4. Pissed off, angry, yelling, annoyed, anxious, frustrated; defensive mode
5. Reaction is over the top; heated, angry, yelling, frustrated; defensive mode, not listening to the other person.

Individuals who are anxious tend to function at 3-5 on the scale because of their irrational thought patterns. It is important to learn your thought patterns so you can use the scale to help you reduce your anxiety and eventually react in a healthier manner.

Always remember, whatever method you choose: Revisit the thoughts after you've have time to de-escalate. Your ability to evaluate and have clarity will help you continuously challenge the negative thoughts.

CHAPTER 10

Implementing the Plan

"6+3= 9 but so does 5+4. The way you do things isn't always the only way to do them. Respect other people's way of thinking."
--Unknown

Before you start, check in with the following:

Have you read all the chapters?
Have you answered all the questions in the chapters?

Reminders:

- Accept your anxiety
- Don't fight your anxiety
- Don't tell yourself there is something wrong with you
- Recognize and challenge your thought patterns
- Use "I" statements
- Communicate your feelings/emotions
- Stay focused and avoid bringing "everything else" into the current situation
- Avoid blaming
- Take a 10-minute break (or longer)
- Find your method that works for you
- Express your fears and insecurities: Let the other person know how you feel
- Don't project your own anxiety onto others
- Check in with assumptions and expectations - unless someone tells you otherwise, don't wander into "Worry Land."

Don't expect to be perfect: You are doing your best.

Good luck!

CHAPTER 11

14-Day Anxiety Challenge

"Note to self: Small steps in the right direction are better than big steps in the wrong direction."
--Unknown

Everything you have read has led you to start the 14-day challenge. Why 14 days? Because you don't want this to be a chore and lose interest in it. 14 days is enough time to begin to learn about your anxiety.

You have learned about your anxiety, negative core beliefs, expectations, and irrational thought patterns. You now have the awareness of your anxiety and the tools to challenge your irrational thoughts. The decision of when you decide to challenge your irrational thoughts is up to you, and when you are ready, you will.

Don't assume and expect this to change overnight; it's a life-long journey. Each day is a step forward, and even if you fall a few steps back - keep moving forward.

My own journey with anxiety has changed, and my quality of life is better. It took work and believing in myself to get here, and I'm continuously moving forward.

Each day will get easier. Try not to get overwhelmed with "It's not changing soon enough." It will.

I won't tell you your anxiety will disappear, because in reality, it won't. But it will become easier to work through, to embrace it and accept that this is part of you.

This workbook will help you recognize how far you have come. If needed, it can be used when you find yourself repeating old patterns. Keep moving forward.

It will change for the better.

14-Day Anxiety Challenge

"Never let yesterday use up too much of today."
--Will Rogers

You have arrived at Chapter 11, so are you ready to start your challenge? If you answered yes, **Good Luck.**

Reminder to self:

I have the choice to change when I am ready, and once I am ready to do this I will change. I can live a healthy and happier life because I believe in me, and I can do this!

In this chapter you will find worksheets that will assist you in challenging your core beliefs, expectations, irrational thoughts, and anxiety.

* 14-day log sheets for you to use when a situation arises that has triggered your anxiety.
  > Date the top of the page
  > Answer all the questions
  > This will help you recognize your patterns
  > Will raise awareness of your core beliefs and thought patterns

* 14-day log sheets to use for your logical thought patterns.
  > New thoughts – healthier thoughts (if applicable)
  > Methods you will use
  > Positive word for the day

Extra worksheets:
* A mood chart to track your mood and intensity
  > This is to be completed weekly
  > This log will help you recognize your patterns

* A thought diary to challenge your irrational thoughts

* Notes:
  > Recognize all your hard work
  > Write about how you feel
  > Write what you have learned
  > You can always go back for reinforcement of what you learned

Give yourself a pat on the back – You got this!

"In any given moment we have two options: to step forward into growth or to step back into safety."
--Abraham Maslow

Date _____ _____ _____

Situation / Activating Event:

_____

_____

Level of anxiety experienced:
Scale of 1 - 10 (1 being the least anxious; 10 being the most) _____

Which symptoms did you experience:
- ❏ Muscle tension
- ❏ Irritability
- ❏ Unable to sleep
- ❏ Difficulty concentrating
- ❏ Tired
- ❏ Headaches
- ❏ Restlessness
- ❏ Racing heart
- ❏ Indecisiveness
- ❏ Overthinking
- ❏ Trembling
- ❏ Nervousness
- ❏ Inability not to worry
- ❏ Sweating

Reaction to situation:

_____

Recognized negative core belief that occurred:

_____

Recognized irrational thought pattern that occurred:

_____

Recognized sensory overload that occurred:

_____

Did my expectations play a role in the situation? How?

_____

How was my communication in the situation?

_____

Date _____ _____ _____

"All you can change is yourself, but sometimes that changes everything!"
--Gary W. Goldstein

Negative core belief I will challenge:

_____

_____

_____

New thought patterns I will implement:

_____

_____

_____

Method I will use to challenge my thoughts:

_____

_____

_____

Positive word of the day:

_____

_____

_____

Notes to self:

_____

_____

_____

Date _____ _____ _____

"Reset. Restart. Refocus. As many times as you need to."
--Steve Maraboli

Situation / Activating Event:

_____

_____

Level of anxiety experienced:
Scale of 1 - 10 (1 being the least anxious; 10 being the most) _____

Which symptoms did you experience:
- ❏ Muscle tension
- ❏ Irritability
- ❏ Unable to sleep
- ❏ Difficulty concentrating
- ❏ Tired
- ❏ Headaches
- ❏ Restlessness
- ❏ Racing heart
- ❏ Indecisiveness
- ❏ Overthinking
- ❏ Trembling
- ❏ Nervousness
- ❏ Inability not to worry
- ❏ Sweating

Reaction to situation:

_____

Recognized negative core belief that occurred:

_____

Recognized irrational thought pattern that occurred:

_____

Recognized sensory overload that occurred:

_____

Did my expectations play a role in the situation? How?

_____

How was my communication in the situation?

_____

Date _____ _____ _____

"If you continue to think the way you've always thought, you'll continue to get what you've always got."
--Kevin Trudeau

Negative core belief I will challenge:

_____

_____

_____

New thought patterns I will implement:

_____

_____

_____

Method I will use to challenge my thoughts:

_____

_____

_____

Positive word of the day:

_____

_____

_____

Notes to self:

_____

_____

_____

"The future belongs to those who believe in the beauty of their dreams."
--Eleanor Roosevelt

Situation / Activating Event:

_____

_____

Level of anxiety experienced:
Scale of 1 - 10 (1 being the least anxious; 10 being the most) _____

Which symptoms did you experience:
- ❏ Muscle tension
- ❏ Irritability
- ❏ Unable to sleep
- ❏ Difficulty concentrating
- ❏ Tired
- ❏ Headaches
- ❏ Restlessness
- ❏ Racing heart
- ❏ Indecisiveness
- ❏ Overthinking
- ❏ Trembling
- ❏ Nervousness
- ❏ Inability not to worry
- ❏ Sweating

Reaction to situation:

_____

Recognized negative core belief that occurred:

_____

Recognized irrational thought pattern that occurred:

_____

Recognized sensory overload that occurred:

_____

Did my expectations play a role in the situation? How?

_____

How was my communication in the situation?

_____

Date _____ _____ _____

"Nothing is impossible. The word itself says, 'I'm possible!'"
--Audrey Hepburn

Negative core belief I will challenge:

_____

_____

_____

New thought patterns I will implement:

_____

_____

_____

Method I will use to challenge my thoughts:

_____

_____

_____

Positive word of the day:

_____

_____

_____

Notes to self:

_____

_____

_____

Date _____ _____ _____

Situation / Activating Event:

_____

_____

Level of anxiety experienced:
Scale of 1 - 10 (1 being the least anxious; 10 being the most) _____

Which symptoms did you experience:
- ❏ Muscle tension
- ❏ Irritability
- ❏ Unable to sleep
- ❏ Difficulty concentrating
- ❏ Tired
- ❏ Headaches
- ❏ Restlessness
- ❏ Racing heart
- ❏ Indecisiveness
- ❏ Overthinking
- ❏ Trembling
- ❏ Nervousness
- ❏ Inability not to worry
- ❏ Sweating

Reaction to situation:

_____

Recognized negative core belief that occurred:

_____

Recognized irrational thought pattern that occurred:

_____

Recognized sensory overload that occurred:

_____

Did my expectations play a role in the situation? How?

_____

How was my communication in the situation?

_____

Date _____ _____ _____

"You must tell yourself, 'No matter how hard it is, or hard it gets, I'm going to make it.'
"
--Les Brown

Negative core belief I will challenge:

_____

_____

_____

New thought patterns I will implement:

_____

_____

_____

Method I will use to challenge my thoughts:

_____

_____

_____

Positive word of the day:

_____

_____

_____

Notes to self:

_____

_____

_____

Date _____ _____ _____

"In the middle of difficulty lies opportunity."
--Albert Einstein

Situation / Activating Event:

_____

_____

Level of anxiety experienced:
Scale of 1 - 10 (1 being the least anxious; 10 being the most) _____

Which symptoms did you experience:
- ❑ Muscle tension
- ❑ Irritability
- ❑ Unable to sleep
- ❑ Difficulty concentrating
- ❑ Tired
- ❑ Headaches
- ❑ Restlessness
- ❑ Racing heart
- ❑ Indecisiveness
- ❑ Overthinking
- ❑ Trembling
- ❑ Nervousness
- ❑ Inability not to worry
- ❑ Sweating

Reaction to situation:

_____

Recognized negative core belief that occurred:

_____

Recognized irrational thought pattern that occurred:

_____

Recognized sensory overload that occurred:

_____

Did my expectations play a role in the situation? How?

_____

How was my communication in the situation?

_____

Date _____ _____ _____

"Don't be pushed by your problems. Be led by your dreams."
--Ralph Waldo Emerson

Negative core belief I will challenge:

_____

_____

_____

New thought patterns I will implement:

_____

_____

_____

Method I will use to challenge my thoughts:

_____

_____

_____

Positive word of the day:

_____

_____

_____

Notes to self:

_____

_____

_____

Date _____ _____ _____

"We aren't given a good life or a bad life. We are given a life. It's up to us to make it good or bad."
--Unknown

Situation / Activating Event:

_____

Level of anxiety experienced:
Scale of 1 - 10 (1 being the least anxious; 10 being the most) _____

Which symptoms did you experience:
- ❑ Muscle tension
- ❑ Irritability
- ❑ Unable to sleep
- ❑ Difficulty concentrating
- ❑ Tired
- ❑ Headaches
- ❑ Restlessness
- ❑ Racing heart
- ❑ Indecisiveness
- ❑ Overthinking
- ❑ Trembling
- ❑ Nervousness
- ❑ Inability not to worry
- ❑ Sweating

Reaction to situation:

_____

Recognized negative core belief that occurred:

_____

Recognized irrational thought pattern that occurred:

_____

Recognized sensory overload that occurred:

_____

Did my expectations play a role in the situation? How?

_____

How was my communication in the situation?

_____

Date _____   _____   _____

"The greatest weapon against stress is our ability to choose one thought over another."
--William James

Negative core belief I will challenge:

_____

_____

_____

New thought patterns I will implement:

_____

_____

_____

Method I will use to challenge my thoughts:

_____

_____

_____

Positive word of the day:

_____

_____

_____

Notes to self:

_____

_____

_____

Don't worry - YOU GOT THIS!

Check in with your progress

Some days may still be a challenge and you will get to that better place!

Notes to self:

_____

_____

_____

_____

_____

_____

_____

_____

_____

_____

_____

_____

Don't worry - YOU GOT THIS!

Check in with your progress

Some days may still be a challenge and you will get to that better place!

Notes to self:

_____

_____

_____

_____

_____

_____

_____

_____

_____

_____

_____

_____

_____

Date _____ _____ _____

"Remember, you can't reach what's in front of you until you let go of what's behind you."
--Unknown

Situation / Activating Event:

_____

_____

Level of anxiety experienced:
Scale of 1 - 10 (1 being the least anxious; 10 being the most) _____

Which symptoms did you experience:
- ❏ Muscle tension
- ❏ Irritability
- ❏ Unable to sleep
- ❏ Difficulty concentrating
- ❏ Tired
- ❏ Headaches
- ❏ Restlessness
- ❏ Racing heart
- ❏ Indecisiveness
- ❏ Overthinking
- ❏ Trembling
- ❏ Nervousness
- ❏ Inability not to worry
- ❏ Sweating

Reaction to situation:

_____

Recognized negative core belief that occurred:

_____

Recognized irrational thought pattern that occurred:

_____

Recognized sensory overload that occurred:

_____

Did my expectations play a role in the situation? How?

_____

How was my communication in the situation?

_____

Date _____ _____ _____

"The way we see the problem is the problem."
--Stephen Covey

Negative core belief I will challenge:

_____

_____

_____

New thought patterns I will implement:

_____

_____

_____

Method I will use to challenge my thoughts:

_____

_____

_____

Positive word of the day:

_____

_____

_____

Notes to self:

_____

_____

_____

*"Don't be afraid to start over. This time you're not starting
from scratch, you're starting from experience."*
--Unknown

Situation / Activating Event:

_____

_____

Level of anxiety experienced:
Scale of 1 - 10 (1 being the least anxious; 10 being the most) _____

Which symptoms did you experience:
- ❏ Muscle tension
- ❏ Irritability
- ❏ Unable to sleep
- ❏ Difficulty concentrating
- ❏ Tired
- ❏ Headaches
- ❏ Restlessness
- ❏ Racing heart
- ❏ Indecisiveness
- ❏ Overthinking
- ❏ Trembling
- ❏ Nervousness
- ❏ Inability not to worry
- ❏ Sweating

Reaction to situation:

_____

Recognized negative core belief that occurred:

_____

Recognized irrational thought pattern that occurred:

_____

Recognized sensory overload that occurred:

_____

Did my expectations play a role in the situation? How?

_____

How was my communication in the situation?

_____

Date _____ _____ _____

"Every day is a new opportunity to change your life."
--Unknown

Negative core belief I will challenge:

_____

_____

_____

New thought patterns I will implement:

_____

_____

_____

Method I will use to challenge my thoughts:

_____

_____

_____

Positive word of the day:

_____

_____

_____

Notes to self:

_____

_____

_____

Date _____ _____ _____

"Well done is better than well said."
--Benjamin Franklin

Situation / Activating Event:

_____

_____

Level of anxiety experienced:
Scale of 1 - 10 (1 being the least anxious; 10 being the most) _____

Which symptoms did you experience:
- ❏ Muscle tension
- ❏ Irritability
- ❏ Unable to sleep
- ❏ Difficulty concentrating
- ❏ Tired
- ❏ Headaches
- ❏ Restlessness
- ❏ Racing heart
- ❏ Indecisiveness
- ❏ Overthinking
- ❏ Trembling
- ❏ Nervousness
- ❏ Inability not to worry
- ❏ Sweating

Reaction to situation:

_____

Recognized negative core belief that occurred:

_____

Recognized irrational thought pattern that occurred:

_____

Recognized sensory overload that occurred:

_____

Did my expectations play a role in the situation? How?

_____

How was my communication in the situation?

_____

Date _____   _____   _____

"Don't get upset with people or situations; both are powerless without your reaction."
--Unknown

Negative core belief I will challenge:

_____

_____

_____

New thought patterns I will implement:

_____

_____

_____

Method I will use to challenge my thoughts:

_____

_____

_____

Positive word of the day:

_____

_____

_____

Notes to self:

_____

_____

_____

Date _____   _____   _____

"Don't be afraid to change. You may lose something good, and you may gain something better."
--Unknown

Situation / Activating Event:

_____

_____

Level of anxiety experienced:
Scale of 1 - 10 (1 being the least anxious; 10 being the most) _____

Which symptoms did you experience:
- ❑   Muscle tension
- ❑   Irritability
- ❑   Unable to sleep
- ❑   Difficulty concentrating
- ❑   Tired
- ❑   Headaches
- ❑   Restlessness
- ❑   Racing heart
- ❑   Indecisiveness
- ❑   Overthinking
- ❑   Trembling
- ❑   Nervousness
- ❑   Inability not to worry
- ❑   Sweating

Reaction to situation:

_____

Recognized negative core belief that occurred:

_____

Recognized irrational thought pattern that occurred:

_____

Recognized sensory overload that occurred:

_____

Did my expectations play a role in the situation? How?

_____

How was my communication in the situation?

_____

Date _____ _____ _____

"Do not learn how to react. Learn how to respond!"
--Buddha

Negative core belief I will challenge:

_____

_____

_____

New thought patterns I will implement:

_____

_____

_____

Method I will use to challenge my thoughts:

_____

_____

_____

Positive word of the day:

_____

_____

_____

Notes to self:

_____

_____

_____

Date _____ _____ _____

Situation / Activating Event:

_____

_____

Level of anxiety experienced:
Scale of 1 - 10 (1 being the least anxious; 10 being the most) _____

Which symptoms did you experience:
- ❏ Muscle tension
- ❏ Irritability
- ❏ Unable to sleep
- ❏ Difficulty concentrating
- ❏ Tired
- ❏ Headaches
- ❏ Restlessness
- ❏ Racing heart
- ❏ Indecisiveness
- ❏ Overthinking
- ❏ Trembling
- ❏ Nervousness
- ❏ Inability not to worry
- ❏ Sweating

Reaction to situation:

_____

Recognized negative core belief that occurred:

_____

Recognized irrational thought pattern that occurred:

_____

Recognized sensory overload that occurred:

_____

Did my expectations play a role in the situation? How?

_____

How was my communication in the situation?

_____

Date _____ _____ _____

"Life is 10% of what happens to you, and 90% of how you react to it."
--Charles R. Swindoll

Negative core belief I will challenge:

_____

_____

_____

New thought patterns I will implement:

_____

_____

_____

Method I will use to challenge my thoughts:

_____

_____

_____

Positive word of the day:

_____

_____

_____

Notes to self:

_____

_____

_____

"Train your mind to see the good in every situation."
--Unknown

Situation / Activating Event:

_____

_____

Level of anxiety experienced:
Scale of 1 - 10 (1 being the least anxious; 10 being the most) _____

Which symptoms did you experience:
- ❏ Muscle tension
- ❏ Irritability
- ❏ Unable to sleep
- ❏ Difficulty concentrating
- ❏ Tired
- ❏ Headaches
- ❏ Restlessness
- ❏ Racing heart
- ❏ Indecisiveness
- ❏ Overthinking
- ❏ Trembling
- ❏ Nervousness
- ❏ Inability not to worry
- ❏ Sweating

Reaction to situation:

_____

Recognized negative core belief that occurred:

_____

Recognized irrational thought pattern that occurred:

_____

Recognized sensory overload that occurred:

_____

Did my expectations play a role in the situation? How?

_____

How was my communication in the situation?

_____

Date _____   _____   _____

"The mind is everything. What you think, you become."
--Buddha

Negative core belief I will challenge:

_____

_____

_____

New thought patterns I will implement:

_____

_____

_____

Method I will use to challenge my thoughts:

_____

_____

_____

Positive word of the day:

_____

_____

_____

Notes to self:

_____

_____

_____

Date _____   _____   _____

"You are only human. You don't have to have it together every minute of every day."
--Anne Hathaway

Situation / Activating Event:

_____

_____

Level of anxiety experienced:
Scale of 1 - 10 (1 being the least anxious; 10 being the most) _____

Which symptoms did you experience:
- ❏   Muscle tension
- ❏   Irritability
- ❏   Unable to sleep
- ❏   Difficulty concentrating
- ❏   Tired
- ❏   Headaches
- ❏   Restlessness
- ❏   Racing heart
- ❏   Indecisiveness
- ❏   Overthinking
- ❏   Trembling
- ❏   Nervousness
- ❏   Inability not to worry
- ❏   Sweating

Reaction to situation:

_____

Recognized negative core belief that occurred:

_____

Recognized irrational thought pattern that occurred:

_____

Recognized sensory overload that occurred:

_____

Did my expectations play a role in the situation? How?

_____

How was my communication in the situation?

_____

Date _____ _____ _____

"Don't let anyone dull your sparkle."
--Unknown

Negative core belief I will challenge:

_____

_____

_____

New thought patterns I will implement:

_____

_____

_____

Method I will use to challenge my thoughts:

_____

_____

_____

Positive word of the day:

_____

_____

_____

Notes to self:

_____

_____

_____

Date _____ _____ _____

"You're not too old, and it's not too late."
--Unknown

Situation / Activating Event:

_____

_____

Level of anxiety experienced:
Scale of 1 - 10 (1 being the least anxious; 10 being the most) _____

Which symptoms did you experience:
- ❏ Muscle tension
- ❏ Irritability
- ❏ Unable to sleep
- ❏ Difficulty concentrating
- ❏ Tired
- ❏ Headaches
- ❏ Restlessness
- ❏ Racing heart
- ❏ Indecisiveness
- ❏ Overthinking
- ❏ Trembling
- ❏ Nervousness
- ❏ Inability not to worry
- ❏ Sweating

Reaction to situation:

_____

Recognized negative core belief that occurred:

_____

Recognized irrational thought pattern that occurred:

_____

Recognized sensory overload that occurred:

_____

Did my expectations play a role in the situation? How?

_____

How was my communication in the situation?

_____

Date _____ _____ _____

"One day you'll look back and realize how hard it was, and just how well you did."
--Charlie Mackesy

Negative core belief I will challenge:

_____

_____

_____

New thought patterns I will implement:

_____

_____

_____

Method I will use to challenge my thoughts:

_____

_____

_____

Positive word of the day:

_____

_____

_____

Notes to self:

_____

_____

_____

Don't worry - YOU GOT THIS!

Check in with your progress

Some days may still be a challenge and you will get to that better place!

Notes to self:

_____

_____

_____

_____

_____

_____

_____

_____

_____

_____

_____

_____

Don't worry - YOU GOT THIS!

Check in with your progress

Some days may still be a challenge and you will get to that better place!

Notes to self:

_____

_____

_____

_____

_____

_____

_____

_____

_____

_____

_____

_____

_____

Mood Log

Week of _____

"The best way of learning about anything is by doing."
--Richard Branson

This worksheet will help you further recognize how you are feeling. Rate your mood at the end of each day.

Scale of 1 - 10

0---5--10

1 - 2: Calm, no impact; minimal reaction

3 - 4: Situation has you elevated, start to become defensive; tone gets louder, body language presents as guarded, angry, frustrated, anxious

5: Frustrated, annoyed; defensive mode

6 - 10: Anxiety is high, reaction is over the top; heated, angry, yelling, frustrated; defensive mode

Date	Anxiety	Irrational Thought

Mood Log

Week of _____

"A negative mind will never give you a positive life."
--Unknown

This worksheet will help you further recognize how you are feeling. Rate your mood at the end of each day.

Scale of 1 - 10

0---5---10

1 - 2: Calm, no impact; minimal reaction

3 - 4: Situation has you elevated, start to become defensive; tone gets louder, body language presents as guarded, angry, frustrated, anxious

5: Frustrated, annoyed; defensive mode

6 - 10: Anxiety is high, reaction is over the top; heated, angry, yelling, frustrated; defensive mode

Date	Anxiety	Irrational Thought

Thought Diary

The situation	What negative thought did you have	Choose an alternative healthy thought

Advantages of your negative thought patterns:

_____

_____

_____

_____

_____

Disadvantages of your negative thought patterns:

_____

_____

_____

_____

_____

Thought Diary

The situation	What negative thought did you have	Choose an alternative healthy thought

Advantages of your negative thought patterns:

_____

_____

_____

_____

_____

Disadvantages of your negative thought patterns:

_____

_____

_____

_____

_____

Handling the Emotional Stuff:
Thoughts, Doodles, and Diversions

In this section you will find pages for writing (or drawing) your own thoughts, and for coloring. Coloring induces a state of meditation, which can be helpful for individuals with anxiety by reducing persistent thoughts.

Blank

Blank

Blank

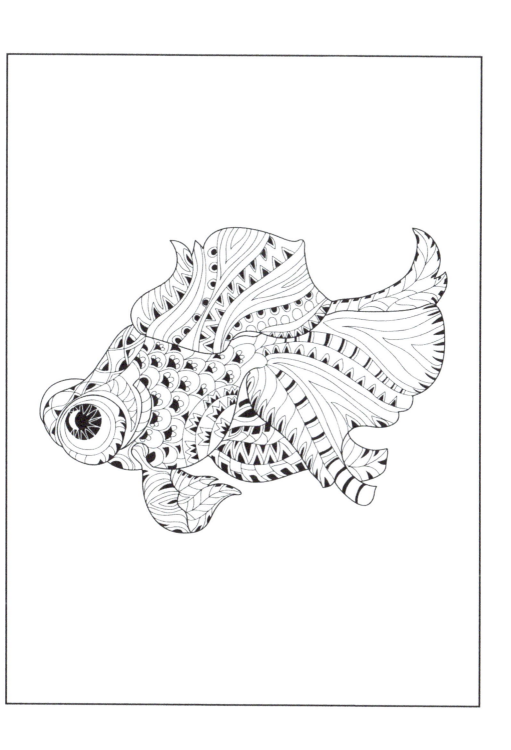

My Thoughts, Doodles, and Diversions

Coping with your upsetting feelings and stress:

When you experience an upsetting feeling, there are steps you can take to reduce the intensity. What are some things you do, and could do, to reduce the feelings? What you do: What you can do instead:

My Thoughts, Doodles, and Diversions

Coping with your upsetting feelings and stress:

When you experience an upsetting feeling, there are steps you can take to reduce the intensity. What are some things you do, and could do, to reduce the feelings? What you do: What you can do instead:

My Thoughts, Doodles, and Diversions

Coping with your upsetting feelings and stress:

When you experience an upsetting feeling, there are steps you can take to reduce the intensity. What are some things you do, and could do, to reduce the feelings? What you do: What you can do instead:

My Thoughts, Doodles, and Diversions

Coping with your upsetting feelings and stress:

When you experience an upsetting feeling, there are steps you can take to reduce the intensity. What are some things you do, and could do, to reduce the feelings? What you do: What you can do instead:

My Thoughts, Doodles, and Diversions

Coping with your upsetting feelings and stress:

When you experience an upsetting feeling, there are steps you can take to reduce the intensity. What are some things you do, and could do, to reduce the feelings? What you do: What you can do instead:

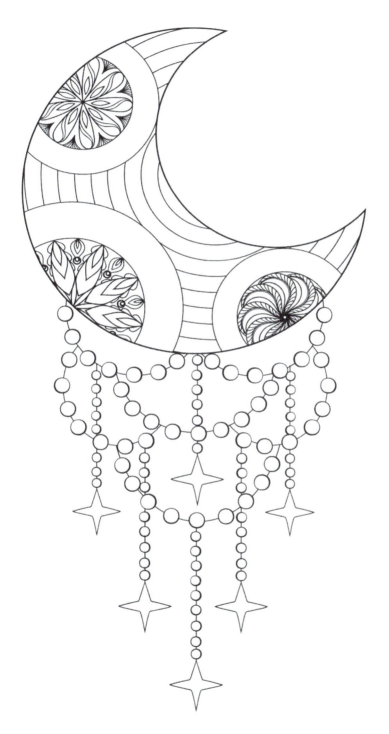

My Thoughts, Doodles, and Diversions

Coping with your upsetting feelings and stress:

When you experience an upsetting feeling, there are steps you can take to reduce the intensity. What are some things you do, and could do, to reduce the feelings? What you do: What you can do instead:

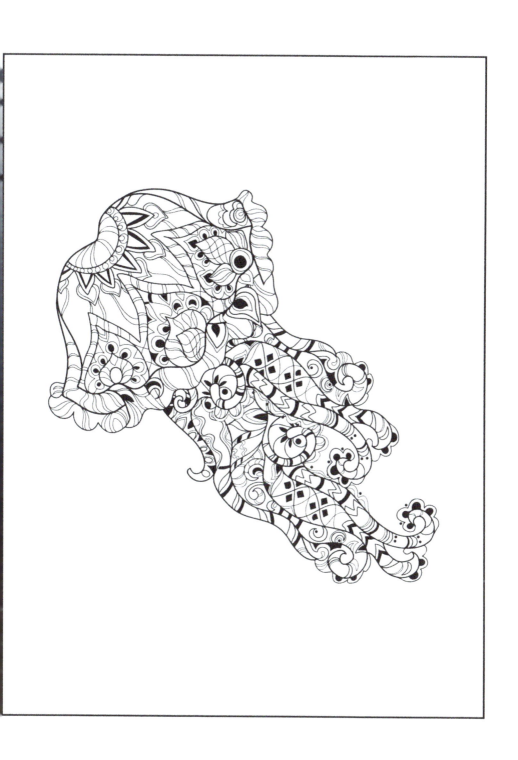

My Thoughts, Doodles, and Diversions

Coping with your upsetting feelings and stress:

When you experience an upsetting feeling, there are steps you can take to reduce the intensity. What are some things you do, and could do, to reduce the feelings? What you do: What you can do instead:

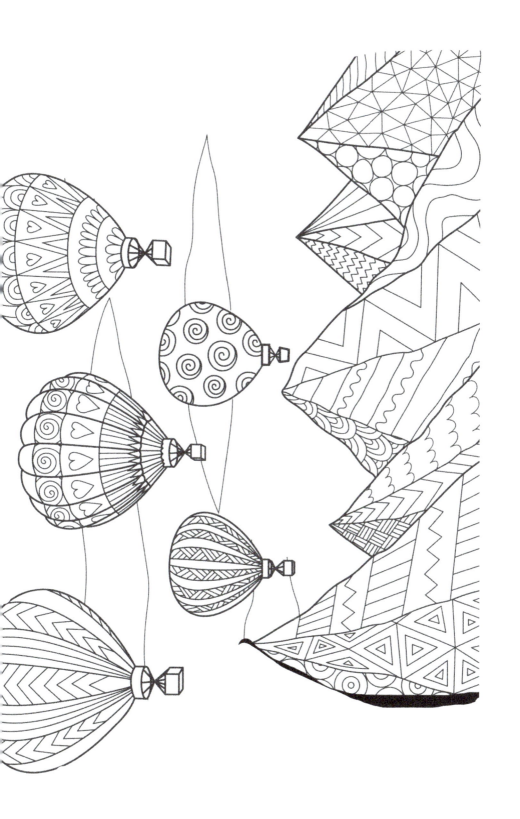

My Thoughts, Doodles, and Diversions

Coping with your upsetting feelings and stress:

When you experience an upsetting feeling, there are steps you can take to reduce the intensity. What are some things you do, and could do, to reduce the feelings? What you do: What you can do instead:

"Be strong, be fearless, and believe anything is possible."
--Unknown

Notes:

_____

_____

_____

_____

_____

_____

_____

_____

Positive word of the day:

_____

_____

_____

"The way I see it, if you want the rainbow, you gotta put up with the rain."
--Dolly Parton

Notes:

_____

_____

_____

_____

_____

_____

_____

_____

_____

_____

Positive word of the day:

_____

_____

_____

"Note to self: I choose not to be defined by my weakness, but by my strength."
--Unknown

Notes:

_____

_____

_____

_____

_____

_____

_____

_____

_____

Positive word of the day:

_____

_____

_____

Notes to self:

"Mistakes are a fact of life. It is the response to the errors that counts."
--Nikki Giovanni

Notes:

_____

_____

_____

_____

_____

_____

_____

_____

_____

_____

_____

_____

Notes to self:

When needed

Reset and restart

References

American Psychiatric Association, Diagnostic and Statistical Manual for Mental Disorders, DSM-5 (2013) APA Press; 5th Edition

Corcoran & Fisher, (2007). *Measures for Clinical Practice and Research*: A Sourcebook. NY, NY; Oxford University Press

Corey, G (2017). *Theory and Practice of Counseling and Psychotherapy*. Boston, MA: Cengage Learning

Curran, L. A. (2013). *101 trauma-informed interventions: Activities, exercises and assignments for moving the client and therapy forward*. Eau Claire, WI: PESI

Johnston, D. W., & Johnston, M. (2001). *Comprehensive clinical psychology*. Amsterdam: Elsevier

Kress, V.E., & Paylo, M.J. (2014), *Treating those with mental disorders; A comprehensive approach to case conceptualization and treatment*. New York, NY: Pearson

Reichenberg, Lourie W., & Seligman, Linda. (2016). *Selecting Effective Treatments*. A comprehensive Systematic Guide to Treating Mental Disorders, Hoboken, NJ: Wiley

Rosenthal, H. (2006). *Therapy's best:* Practical advice and gems of wisdom from twenty accomplished counselors and therapists. New York: Haworth Press

Roth, A., Fonagy, P., (2005), *What Works for Whom?* Second Edition; A Critical Review of Psychotherapy Research, NY: Guilford Press

Sammons, M & Schmidt, N. (eds.) (2001). *Combined Treatments for Mental Disorders,* Washington D.C.: American Psychological Press

Made in the USA
Monee, IL
24 June 2023

37177500R00066